MISS AMERICA

FENCEbooks

Gerhard Richter, German, b. 1932, *Woman Descending the Staircase,* 1965, oil on canvas, 200.7 x 129.5 cm., Roy J. and Frances R. Friedman Endowment; Gift of Lannan Foundation, 1997.176 The Art Institute of Chicago. All Rights Reserved.

Published in the United States by   Fence Books
                                          14 Fifth Avenue, #1A
                                          New York, NY 10011
                                          www.fencebooks.com

Book design by   Saturnalia Books

Printed in Canada by   Westcan Printing Group

Fence Books is distributed by   University Press of New England
                                          www.upne.com

Library of Congress Cataloguing in Publication Data
         Wagner, Catherine [1969–]
         Miss America / Catherine Wagner

Library of Congress Control Number: 2001093170

ISBN 0-9663324-7-4

FIRST EDITION

Portions of this book appeared in slightly different form as the chapbooks *Hotel Faust,* from West House Books, and *Fraction Anthems,* from 811 Books. Many poems in this book were first published in the following magazines: *Colorado Review, Denver Quarterly, Explosive, Faucheuse, Fence, Gare du Nord, Interim, Iowa Review, Longhost, Ribot,* and *Skanky Possum.* The author is very grateful to the editors.

For my parents

TABLE OF CONTENTS

All Bar One

nigh said I made that up to
get some sweeteye from you all
some glance at me even if my
story is boring and a lie
nigh am so sick of doubting
myself an thinking I am bad
nigh bore myself
anyway trying to be like the udders
and who fuckin cares they don't
want me to be likem and borem
everybody dead.
Since I been here SCARED
and my natural EBULLISHNESS
held back by a warning finger.
Mo lady! Poop it out!
They lovit run yawling
scared and come back for more.
My natural LOVE tucked into
DESIRE I am folded into
envelope just hoping to
receive some love from the
eyes bent away bent
now but Unfold the flaps
and be a Page girl to the World

MAGAZINE POEMS

A Poem for *Nature*

       Yellow is a word for diving
       That turned sideways   into a diamond

Will you express a certain amount of liquid loss
Will you cabinet that
And make sure red silk
And taboo that
And ease on the plasters
I was blonde when I said
       Fill the roots in

My transformation while
I don't know what happens
In my spine or exactly
My bowels
       Gully lady
Methane
Coming out, and petroleum
Semi-solids
Applied, and perhaps worn

There are other sorts of
Liquid but you could even
Call them loss

A Poem for *Guideposts*

I made a pie of light
Sat me down in front
The glaze sucked all the blue out of the air
I was a pilot search
Went intrinsically backward
The moss of my feet booked me in
Moss and wet cloud
I held my spine up natural head natural like a top spins
Will God deny me anything
God will I eat a piece of the world
Piece of gone
There was a streaming wedge but it was not a piece it was
The whole boat
It was carried
Our shoulders dirt our shoulders smell like come
Swerve round this round that balancedly
The one plate and the other at varying levels till the table comes

A Poem for *Poets & Writers*

I always want to begin with if
Usually reject it
Plunge in solid I reverse myself
If because what I say is mutable
If can't be rubbed out really

march march march march march march

And in the absence there is a form to be filled out
A forum or group work
You order
I run and get the food
You give me some money
Some could not read this
It would be like reading

       tentacles
       your eyes

which has meaning
I hate not understanding
I like understanding so much I want it to happen over and over

A Poem for *Time*

Deem this well, deem me into a great
                                        poof of light

Preface
I love you very much

Introduction
Oh jeez riding inside it
Under the eye of me gaping a room
O hi riding inside it
Outside the belly a larger balloon
Dear friends

Ancilla
That is damage talk
I don't know it
All but there isn't
Anything else
Want to watch me
Make it

A Poem for *Art in America*

Rattle it rattle it

Goddamn box-elder bugs

I am thinking of my future
So can't write a poem

Pee, pee   low   low
That is how the song upstairs goes

Scary Ligeti music doesn't cover it up

Not here with joy but under pressure
            from my superego

Hey I have not had my tea yet
Leave me alone

filled up my mind with a long stroke of
Dependence and left it wriggling

Hearken awhile from thy greene cabinet

A Poem for *Social Text*

My ears can hear in any direction but my eyes see 180°
I was thinking that Clinton was a moderate Democrat
I didn't use any words to think it because I was in Heaven
I was clear
Their mean vibrations had nothing
Through which to reverb
I was so OK

Café Rouge

Webby tree
Please do to me
Inside of cage thing
Spreading wooden finger thing
Shoulderblades frayed the cloth I'm made of
Sewn up my neck round speaking hole
and ragged with snot
pale salmon concealer sodden
I pick and pick the seam all day
does I really think anything covers me up
this my swan is it
eyes at one end cunt at the other
a swaying hurting wonder between
which is posture perfect

More glamorough
more pretooty

This is the way to the hall with the priest-holes Cathy

Bleak Apt

Even supposing—they can very well do without much beauty
in me. —Do you ever look in the glass?

Zip zip zip endlessly teeth brushing
Guilt does not stop me from one bad thing I do.
When you get close-to you'll find I am very critical and know best about everything
I am so afraid I'll snot when I laugh I get all squinched.
If you stand there like that it makes me nervous and I'll never be ready and I'll
        forget something.

I went down to the end of the bed
I thought I would hug his feet, they were chilly and faintly vinegary
then I remembered to feel like I was chickenwire exposed to the world unknown
Oooh. My eyes have stung all day like I've been to a movie
Rusting
My neck and jaws are tense, I feel them quiver slightly
Now if I could move around, toss in bed and down street
and still sense the entering there I'd be

You smelled my balls—you were touching my balls.
I'll leave you in peace. I can't believe I said that.
What.
I leave you in peace.
Why.
That was my grandmother's suicide note.
Your grandmother's here. She's hovering an inch over your face
screaming into your face.
Stop it.
Sorry. She's two inches away from your face.

Crow

for Ric, Ann and Lucy Caddel

When I don't know thing about him
Which I don't
Quit lying here thinking he's around
Hello
When it's alcohol speeding up the blood
How dare feel bad don't know
Just best wishes etc, and carefully
Drunk and thirsty I have filled my water bottle
And have to pee
No absence round me
Reckon them up
Not often in the dawn
Everybody in his slot her slot
And my love for them
And bad ungrateful thoughts or not
How many glorious cells in big Martin
tuck my leg to his loins
Shed on me
Thy grace and little cells and smells
And everyone else absent
Mom, Dad, curlygirl
I do too have emotion
little Emma Annamarie
dear Wendy and Rebecca

Angie who I begoned from me
or come down from acid with Robby in dun
gray and silken rising
my own flesh which was in a passage
it said 5:33 I was come back
from getting water
If any of you die I don't know
I'll kill you bunch of
Pretend you left me for dead
Then I am good enough and loved you enough
Please shut up now
The sky now available through the curtains
Going to say the curtains now in flower
Without my glasses blue
Through squiggled translucent red
Tom I am not worthy to receive
Only say the word
And you are still yours
Which is the human lock
Achieved a moral there
I can fuck off though
Because I don't know
Sweet sweet sweet sweet sweet sweet sweet
That is a sparrow and good morning my love

MAGAZINE POEMS

A Poem for *Good Housekeeping* (after Wittgenstein)

Of course, that is a bus such as I have often seen on Third Avenue.

From inside one transports oneself with it until one is there.

Of course, that is a book such as I have often seen on the dining-room table.

One reserves marks with it until they mean or not.

One has various reasons.

Of course that is a mother such as I have often seen in my childhood.

One mothers oneself with it until its end of the equation.

Of course, that is a boyfriend such as I have often seen sleeping.

One reassures oneself with it until one leaves for work.

A Poem for *Marketplace*

I can't see the cars
Human riding on the sound

All press forward with a mute over their strings
For a moment there were no cars

God I love that noise

A person strapped in warm and going

They are all going to work

I think it is nice that they all go
Recalcitrant surge

Left the definite Indian behind

A Poem for *Harper's Bazaar*

Black caw gimme a gnaw
I wore your underclothes
Walked to the river and soaked my toe
Down to the undergrow
Nail gone, go callus, bonepull, raw
You been eating too much too fast
You fat and gassy and tepid
You been silver and gold, you match
You plaid metal up to the neckbridge

And I I say been belted round
With Virginia creeper
And I been choked down marrow out
And fed tinfoil till bloated

We all sat round and watched TV
That evening
You had a cigarette the smoke was your halo

      Little storm in the skin
      Rushes out
      Bright house

If I had a girl

Who would speak through her gun
If I had a print
Of a coo or a caw

A pale plaid print
On a jubbly thigh
A mayonnaise face
And a switch of rouge

        La loony boyette
doot doot doot   doot doot doot
la loony.

A Poem for *Aperture* (Beloved)

Why don't you empty
Little garden
Empty your kerchief

Only a couple of hours in the sun
Your closet plant will turn green
One giant rode on the other side of you

One giant rode on the one side of you
One was trying to kiss your ear
And the other one ignored you

I kept to the side of you
Ran round and kissed the giant
Tall gold filter

Tallest of cowboys
I have the outside of your house
And a path in your toothbrush bristles

White renaissance garden
Cleanly
Your little kerchief

WHITE MAN POEMS

I

My lover is a white man
Who else
My daddy
Who else.
The president is going to be impeached.
Some white men let me tell them what to do.
I said to one cut half these poems out your manuscript.
He is so grateful!
Wait for the white man to pick me up either in a station wagon
        or a blue van.
White man half an hour late!
I have been faithful to you white-man-area in my fashion.
        Ernest Dowson
That sounds like an early twentieth-century black man but it is a
        nineteenth-century white man.
Smell of an old sock
His anus smell like an old dollar bill
But you can't just have a little something on the side

II

You have to feel sorry for them
You have to feel sorry for them

But I am, I am one.
They don't know that.
They let me drive their car.
If I was President,
NONSTOP LICKY
I'm afraid I can't think without licky
White man wrote almost every book in that shelf
Some nice guys
I sit with them, make healthy sonnet-juice
What are Jews are they all the way white?
The Jews spring to mind

III

Am not required to praise, required to love I am

Praise for him falls short of what himself can give

I ask a lot, and so I do receive from him

I ask nothing, and nothing do I gain of him
He asks nothing

Lie down now in cold blanket having bitchy thoughts
Aggression will out here or it will out elsewhere
He knows he's meant to keep the phone away from me
(My sister, come to town, she doesn't trust me much)

Sounds like he's going to keep the phone away from me

Must write poems to fill the huge demand for them

This Land is Your Land

This Land is Island
This land is europe
Aslant of plain air
I knew your prophecy
A frozen farway
Paradisiacal
This iceland made for you and me

Iceland is I land a secret green land
A holy thighland
Running green glass water
I new above me
You knew below me
We heard of liberty
Inside till cracked bell rings
Heard your skin inside me
This love all round you
In a whole pink pocket
Beat in my shoulders
Tide round my sacrum
Don't know what you are
Don't know what that is
Is all coming up me
Is all approaching

Rest in the stiff soft mat of chest
Stiff soft line
Soft active
Stiff soft act
My dear all round me
Reproach, reproach,
Reproach, and weep and shelter
Animal in shell posse how many are you
All around me like a tree
Tighten and darting nerve your face
Died on the plane
Give me plain air
I am so dirty
I am not you
My pilot crushed
Reignite island burn up
Fact died in dilate
Make a pen rise a
Keyboard depress elbow on it

jhhhhhhhhh
Die and I know what to do comfort
Live and I fucking don't know
New in my house
Put me in jail

Under hill put out my eyes
I am shopping
Sing for 80 years until I wrinkle up
And dry to you
Was my wedding precise
Was my wedding nice
Kiss you without the skin on
My whole house is drunk
Monday 6 PM man deplane through tube
In my land
If it is gorgeous if it is yours

When I Asked You to Marry Me

I hoped
pink skin, pink skin not ready
          yet for me

soaped the braincase with the question
my love winters in a capsule

a lion wall
I am disturbing you am I
I am punch punch punch punch
Dame Mortifie does not call her friends
because you are here and that is enough

Clogs me enough
       Birds already starting
I won't go to our party, I'll
hide in the street
slovenly
save a little money and move to New York. I want that
Skin gets rubbly. Pores like mom's, and body
please calm, honey, all happens however you feel about it
a little while ago walked past window reflected
what's wrong with me, awake
again and anxious how many times—

I do this and have done this and will
I am awake at a vague strange point
How exciting! Popcorn at 5
in the morn, going to read
a novel, and the sprinklers start
Bird bash beak on the window

What doing, crazy bird?
Grosbeak sees itself in the window
Sofa illimitably tolerant of me

I Am Darling You

let me king around
you king all over, mighty

Bring a town in, okay,
add a country,

slavish all over me, please.

Darned mighty, sleeping,
oyster eyes.

Feel little. Little my head to sleep.

I suffer you, you basic.

Deign down, lean at me, chosen.

Judas Icarus.

He made enough for me to take to lunch.

MAGAZINE POEMS

Two Poems for *Entertainment Weekly*

1

If you are Gwyneth
You are never toenails on my rug
Abounding
From west to east
I see my self walk west in the windows
You are Clinton or Nixon
And get your hair cut often
A tribe indulging
At work I am considered
Introverted and thus intelligent and flaky
Indulged
A vision you are like farmers
Sow grow pluck
Of the hair of millions
Linda Evangelista's hair
Was meant to be eaten
This is her body which was given
This hair page two
Hey fatface—mommylove—
Caramel sweetfuck hair

2

Scout and Rumor suck me off
We will flower inside you like a dog at your 'trails
I am sorry
Just a gigolo
Friendly and forsaken
Is it hotter to wear a bra
Or let my boobs stick to my chest
Melanin, melatonin, metonym, melanoma

A Poem for ESPN (Nightwatchman)

When he went for the free-throw
There had been waking that morning
And in a soup of grease bubbles
Bacon
A long and merciful shit
Somebody sing it again kings and queens
Troubadour spells trouble
Wet trousers of nightfall
I loved him, sailor
Eyebrows a burned swath in the rainforest
Of his zits
When he went for the free-throw
Sailor redempt me
The inside of the basket
In somebody's hands sir
Redempt my solitariness

A Poem for Sears Roebuck

Is there a Kenmore, Penny Kenmore for ex
Or maybe it means "extremely canny"
I wrote a joke postcard first time in New York
Age 16 —"I've been discovered
As Pretty Plus model for Sears catalog"
I did not think I was
That tubby
But friend believed me
That is a bad lagoon, fat girl lagoon
I am wearing Husky Boys cutoffs
Wrangler
Sears no longer carry 1) carpenter pants
2) workmens overalls 3) Beefy T's by Hanes
I don't know who does sell the last anymore

A Poem for *Cosmopolitan*

to Thomas Hart Benton

I said, Ba-by
He came in a rush
Can you be more specific
Not with a cottonball but maybe with a Q-tip
Horrif, horrif, she howled—Horrif.

A Poem for *Poetry*

The Wallace Stevens investigation
X'ed out his lungs
Hu—Huh—Huh
Cl—ck—his whole throat sealed up
The dam busted, it was like Vladimir with a sword
His Highlander calves clenched
As if beanbags were sewn in
His tongue sweated
A little rainy-foggy, nice and moist
The definite plasma spun off
Huh—hh—hulp—huh

FRACTION ANTHEMS

FRACTION ANTHEM[1]

Delver: There was a place in the brain,
a red knot. We live in there, we play seek.
We live in there, we ratchet.
Blitzkrieg. We peony.
Will you come out of there, take my
stringy bloody sinew pulse hand

       Say goodbye to HER

she make you lie, don't love

And a rock feels no pain, dingle dingle

ding, and an island.

I am sexually attracted

to him, he gets on my nerves, she

jealous of me, I think she's clever, love

my boyfriend. Bowl the fucking ball.

I poured it full of foam.

Goddamn I hate mole, cat-hair on
my black pants.

Catarrh.
river cut, air cut. My thighfat, my gullet,
stringed down, scuttle.
My thermometer wilt. Go trade.

FRACTION ANTHEM²

Felix girls:

I[f] put out a new shoot

We   —the teapot clarks—

Navy strip over
blue white horiz, oh
red yellow GREEN plaid
[We await Steve]
rug.   Good, I am full, I made pasta
            Smoke   Foot
 Throw.   *beeper*   his knee
            his foot   *airplane*   *car*   his elbow

        P   his foot
          O   my   blue snub
         E   knee   weekend
          thumbnail
       hand M
            foot   "I work"
)Lamp

                                        —10:30 Sat morn—

                                        "it's sugar day

44

FRACTION ANTHEM[3]

That's the one on whose side I love you all night long

ace the open road
in hairpins
Delight! Oh rare.
The French equivalent of that

He was a kisser   KISSER
He had a mouth to give
His mouth was mobile and he had crooked teeth

FRACTION ANTHEM[4]

Girl, you have gorgeous skin, milkbottle skin,
I am so afraid
I lift your little skirt but you have leggings on

Sleep
S'gone gray. I was out in the pretty part.
Only at the bus stop.
Things divide other things, real life

I am after enjoyment.

I clench my cupful I forgot about my cupful
I think you only know it because it is attention doing it
Or afterward, it was attention
I love subservience—Little shine, you are grown
I don't know what you are, significance, bled hand
In Idaho, dumpling in the dark, frisson, we fought.
I slept with you every fucking night, four years.
Idaho queensize, you're weird, cold milk
(my stomach turned) hairy. I guess we made up.
—She walked on soft and foggy.
Railroad of bobby pins and friendly men in there.
I could go on and on, suspired.
—Loot! Loot!—

Nary day, shined up nice.
Here come Martin

FRACTION ANTHEM[5]

My fraction anthem meets up here
In blue caboose
An anthem frays the bald spot
Totally trails
Totally for others
Say it with fractions
Things divide other things, real life

FRACTION ANTHEM[6]

         my part in raising likelihoods
edge of the bed
I'm sure I forgot somebody's water
I forgot that old man's side of thousand

FRACTION ANTHEM[7]

I clad over the west with my light atrocious
freaked at the lines that go out
from each knuckle-angle,
many a cornice with which to involve oneself
geometrically or in terms of perspective,
radial flush and a frame that is gone next time

Lady,   gets on the bus
          red away

FRACTION ANTHEM[8]

Still asleep in its bunny
the world arrives. Lyre,
pinch, a gale.
                        A pigeon
leaps the furry straits

paint mucked all round the window edges,
bus gone by
no Martin. 2 tiny red bugs
cross the white swoosh. Martin!
Fuzzy round the edges and kinder
than Lance even, or Jeff Clark
Ruddy, and kind   shall I compare you.
first-rate, with a freckle on your temple.

Still asleep in it, honey,
asleep in the bunny.
I will get cold. Demur, with fur.
Get cellulite, and pubes. Morose,
in there, the veinfugue, limited.
Pasted-on formica, winestain bellybutton
rabid nipple, ha.
Why stain. Why

wriggle free of haunches.
Curl up toes, demesne.

Then Martin sit in the car with Chris,
agossip, needing a shave.
Rise bun! Slant home,
good Chris, fogged up,
please send him gesturing in.
Knee clamp, wrist clamp, mine.
Big ol chest, mine, sit by refrigerator,
sleep mouth open, funny. Here minus.
Here he mine come smile.

FRACTION ANTHEM[9]

I knee, knee then knee then knee, knee.
Wulp. Somebody saw.

I 7–11

they milk and mayonnaise
me. God is in me talking. Burble.
God is tired in me. I miss, I miss

and miss. Amply, am-
ply, all keep
up with me easy.

FRACTION ANTHEM[10]

There is a full moon
And the remarks you made are swollen into canisters
Of lucky redolent dynamite
Sweetie
I am casting around

FRACTION ANTHEM[11]

I am groovin, I am after the big whang

Noan so close   (glance)

   crotch here   crotch here
front   front   front   front
down (feet) down   down (feet) down
back   back   back   back

Whoa that's   my left turn
    Flesh hair out
on stairs. Mike morose, cuts lemons
Vivify. Hi Mike! Hello Cathy. 2/4. Versify.

FRACTION ANTHEM[12]

Got out of the car and sang my tendons out, licky happy
Laughed at my own joke and got a bloody nose
Pimply and shiny from work

FRACTION ANTHEM[13]

I would like an elegant
smoke gray suit
or chew gum, wear halter

sit in lawnchair bird shit on me

What is fun?
Nothing is fun
Quit banging
Bent into chill
under blanket   lovegrubb
nice girl

definitely made definitely infinite

I am a tells lies
Head chopped off

veer toward homosexuality which maintains
air of naughtiness also toward
children touch child
touch your own bud wrongly
like come back from dead you

curl into grief
                 ] upload
splay as happy

"Arrange the vowels in their order of darkness"

FRACTION ANTHEM[14]

.

Because it is cold
Because they are fashionably
wide-legged

I thought for a small bag for my
books I can carry comfortably
I don't like it

It is red it doesn't go with my
anorak which is maroon
It is a little too big

Then I found a swell harness

FRACTION ANTHEM[15]

A little bell in the tree, ha ha
It shed on me
A ting and a ting and I saw it not
I sat around in my linen shirt
Beneath the tree on a mat, ha ha
Displeased, and displeased
For I had not worked and I had just sat
And I had not exercised
But to blow a fly off the mat

I remembered Marvell's Garden
Where the drunk falls down on grass
Drunk on grapes or on thinking
And he thinks a peacock thought
He thinks he can think
A bigger than a this
That's to think with a peacock's eyes
The eye is a coin and it sees the realm
The realm it is coin of the realm in
The realm real money
Reflective and exchange
I will have caught the sun sitting here
Drunk on fir.

FRACTION ANTHEM[16]

I was how old I was

exiting theater fear throng

man alone next me

the striped one stinky under arms

what he want
 so dumb movie lone

This approached woman

I tonally split

FRACTION ANTHEM[17]

When I bite sandwich do
I bite evenly   split
middlemeat?
Hold bread still with bottom teeth

cover lower teeth with tongue see
   how upper teeth manage then
would not work to cover top
teeth as this would prevent swallowing

I am sure full of bubbles

clearly

the fundament

must stretch

mine goes Tues Wed Thurs

Fri 96 9/6 Fri 10:46:06

FRACTION ANTHEM[18]

Me encanta division

It is addiction to a path, no

The plucky monarch climbed
the pyramid

The Span Prime Min
 getting keys to Mex City
"Spain has always taken an
enormous interest in Mexico it is
not for nothing it was
called New Spain"

Pressing bruise

"text must literally be the instructions

to physically live"

—all day—& under my stockings

FRACTION ANTHEM[19]

Shine and shine and shine and shine
 [flicker]

where the salt is, which drawer the spoons are in

BLAT!

I am tired of this ugly language

Apple burden my slow jaw
Bird run along missing
Cat landed a-two foot turned

FRACTION ANTHEM[20]

And through it

      spawny all

I'm

—A massive doghead poked in the ajar

it was the landlord's
      Scared it screaming

FRACTION ANTHEM[21]

Smile   climb
  from

PLEASE Hands in Elope into
Push, push Blurry
   the mouth prayer, OK,
inward the
        knock
   my Everybody

NOTES*

¹ANTHEM Delver: red-knot. In-there, live there, we of-there stringy-bloody goodbye HER she feels-no dingle-ding am attracted to of-me she's-clever, the ball. I mole,-cat-hair black-pants. cut. my trade.

²ANTHEM Felix -the-teapot strip-over red GREEN plaid I-made Foot-Throw. foot *car* his E-knee hand-M SAT

³ANTHEM That's all-night the-open Oh The French He-had to-give and had crooked

⁴ANTHEM Girl, so-afraid your-little leggings Sleep S'gone Only-at stop-Things life am after my-cupful you-only is doing it Little-shine, grown-I are bled hand fought.-I you-every Idaho you're weird we-made walked-on of pins and and-on, Loot!—Nary Here Martin

⁵ANTHEM my an-anthem bald-spot others it with

⁶ANTHEM my I'm-sure somebody's-water man's of thousand

⁷ANTHEM I freaked-at that-go many cornice with of-perspective and-a next Lady, gets

8ANTHEM   Still pinch,-a pigeon-leaps   mucked   round the tiny-
red the-white   the   and kinder kind-shall you.-first-rate,   your
Still asleep has-a will-get   Get   and pubes. formica-winestain
nipple,-ha.   free   haunches. Curl car-with needing-a   home
Chris, fogged wrist-clamp ol-chest   sleep   open, funny.

9ANTHEM   I Somebody-saw they-milk   is   me talking. I-miss and-
miss.   keep   with me

10ANTHEM   There made-are canisters-Of   I   casting around

11ANTHEM   I Noan-so crotch-here   front   down (feet) Whoa-
that's turn-Flesh   Mike   cuts lemons

12ANTHEM   Got out,-licky at-my   a   nose Pimply

13ANTHEM   I chew-gum sit-in   me   is fun? Under-blanket girl-
definitely   am   lies Head of-naughtiness children-touch   bud
like come splay-as the vowels

14ANTHEM   Because wide-legged-I a-small   I   carry comfortably
doesn't-go anorak-which   a   big I

15ANTHEM   shed-on ting-and   saw   not I tree-on ha-ha   I   not
worked not-exercised blow-a   I   Marvell's Garden on-grapes

thinking-And   thought   thinks he to-think peacock's-eyes   coin
it sees the-realm realm-real   I   have caught

[16]ANTHEM I throng-man me- the   the   what he I-tonally

[17]ANTHEM When middlemeat?–Hold with-bottom   with   see
how cover-top as-this   I   sure full goes-Tues Fri-96

[18]ANTHEM Me no-The climbed-the   Mex   "Spain has is-
not it-was   bruise   must literally &-under

[19]ANTHEM Shine the-salt drawer-the   I   tired of Bird-run Cat-
landed

[20]ANTHEM And poked-in it-was   screaming

[21]ANTHEM Smile push-Blurry prayer,-OK,   Everybody

*Notes constructed by passing my social security number through
FRACTION ANTHEMS

FENCE was launched in the spring of 1998. A biannual journal of poetry, fiction, art and criticism, **FENCE** has a mission to publish challenging writing and art distinguished by idiosyncrasy and intelligence rather than by allegiance with camps, schools, or cliques.   **FENCE** has published works by some of the most esteemed contemporary writers as well as excellent work by complete unknowns. It is part of our mission to support young writers who might otherwise have difficulty being recognized because their work doesn't "fit in" to either the mainstream or to accepted modes of experimentation.

FENCEbooks is an extension of that mission; with our books we hope to provide expanded exposure to poets and writers whose work is excellent, challenging, and truly original. **The Alberta Prize** is an annual series launched in 2000 by **FENCE**books in conjunction with the Alberta duPont Bonsal Foundation. The Alberta Prize offers publication of a first or second book of poems by a woman, as well as a $5,000 cash prize underwritten by the Alberta duPont Bonsal Foundation.

Our second prize series is the **Fence Modern Poets Series**, published in cooperation with **saturnalia books**. This contest is open to poets of either gender and at any stage in their career, be it a first book or fifth.

For more information about either prize, visit our website at www.fencebooks.com, or send an SASE to **FENCE**books /[Name of Prize], 14 Fifth Avenue, #1A, New York, NY 10011.

To see more about   **FENCE** ,visit www.fencemag.com